HOW
TO GET TO
SCHOOL
IN SIXTY
SECONDS

Gareth P. Jones

Illustrated by Steve May

OXFORD
UNIVERSITY PRESS

Preface

By Hector Cook, age 11

I didn't know what a preface was until Kara May (my neighbour and an actual author) suggested I write one. Apparently a preface is a bit of the story that isn't the actual story but introduces what the story is about. So here is my preface.

This is a book for anyone who has ever had to scramble in the morning to get to school on time. If the school run (as parents call it) involves actual running for you, then you're in the right place. I recommend that you read this book if your parents have ever been known to shout things like:

1. 'You'll need to get dressed quicker than that.'
2. 'Where are my keys?'
3. 'Why haven't you brushed your teeth?'
4. 'I told you to turn that television off.'
5. 'What do you mean, you haven't finished your breakfast yet? What have you been doing?'
6. 'How can you lose a shoe?'

7. 'Could you put that coat on any more slowly?'
8. 'We have to go ... NOW!'

If you don't recognize any of these then you must be one of those people who always allows plenty of time to get to school. All my life, I have envied people like you, but even if you have never experienced the morning mad-flap panic, I hope you still might appreciate this story. It is an account of how – despite all the odds and in the face of serious opposition – we eventually found a way of getting to school in sixty seconds flat.

Chapter 1
The late book

There is a book on our school reception desk where pupils have to record their reasons for being late. Angela, our school receptionist, calls it the Hector Cook Book because my name is Hector Cook and I have to write in it every day. My sister's name, Agnes, appears just as often but she is younger and only writes about imaginary monkeys so it's up to me to fill in our explanations. Here are the last four reasons we were late for school:

1. On the bus my sister screamed, 'There's a monkey sitting on the driver's shoulder!' so loudly that the bus driver made us get off so we had to walk the rest of the way.
2. Mum forgot something but we couldn't get back in because the keys were stuck on the roof, meaning I had to climb in through a window.
3. Kara May called the police to report the sighting of a giant snake in her back garden, meaning Mum had to hang around to 'answer questions about it'.
4. Mum flooded the kitchen with yogurt, then Agnes decided to use my shoes to scoop it out.

Reading this list back, it is clear to me that the main reasons for me being late involve:

1. my sister
2. my mum
3. a lethal combination of them both.

Hmm, I have realized that there are already numerous things that you need to understand about my family even though we haven't got to the story yet. Here are five of them:

1. There are four members of our family: Dad (Rob), Mum (Sally), my sister (Agnes) and me.
2. Dad's job means he has to leave for work very early and arrive home very late so he's really only good for weekends and the occasional bedtime.

DAD (ROB)

Bags under eyes

SUIT (works in sales)

ALARM CLOCK (has to be up early)

MUM (SALLY)

Invents things

Works from home

Hasn't made any money (yet)

3. Mum works from home, although I'm not sure it counts as actual work since she's an inventor and none of her inventions have ever made any money. Whenever I say this to her she always replies, 'Yet', as if to imply that her inventions 'haven't made any money yet'. But that's the same as saying Baby Marky next door hasn't turned into a hippopotamus yet. Because he's never going to, is he?

4. Agnes is five years old and the randomest person on the planet. (Yes, I know randomest isn't a real word but my neighbour Kara May told me that real writers make up words all the time. She has been helping me write my story but I'll explain more about that later.)

5. I'm Hector. I'm 11 years old and I like making lists.

MY SISTER
(AGNES)
Randomest person on the planet!!
Age 5

ME
(HECTOR)
Age 11
LIST
Likes making lists

Lists help me make sense of things and when your mum is a zany inventor and your sister is the queen of randomness, you need something to help you make sense of things.

My idea was to write this story entirely as lists (except for these bits in between when I'm telling you what's going on and preparing to introduce the next list). I didn't know if it was a good idea so I asked Kara May, who is a writer in real life and has actual books with her name on. She said, 'I've never heard of anyone doing it but I can't see why it wouldn't be possible. In fact, yes, it would probably be quite interesting. It might make certain bits tricky though.'

I then asked her about making up words but you know what she said about that. I've discovered it's not straightforward to write a story in a sensible order. Since this story (which is all true) is about how to get to school in sixty seconds flat I'd better give you an idea of how difficult that would be, so here are five observations about our journey to school:

1. Our house is around one and a half miles from school (or 2414 metres to be precise).
2. We have a car but Dad uses it to get to work.

3. Agnes, Mum and I walk an average of three miles an hour. I know this sounds slow, but it includes stopping time caused by my sister shouting at trees, or the lollipop lady refusing to let us cross the road. (More on both of those later.)

4. If you're any good at maths you will already have worked out that this means it takes us thirty minutes to walk to school. (I'm not going to show my workings so you'll just have to do the equation yourself.)

5. School starts at 08.55 am so if we leave the house at 08.25 am we can make it on time. (We never do.)

6. There is a bus, which theoretically stops at 08.35 am and should speed up our journey by ten minutes, but sometimes it's late and sometimes it's early so it can't really be relied on.

Chapter 2
Mum's inventions

Writing a story isn't as easy as I thought. It turns out there are lots of essential pieces of information which aren't actually part of the main story. I asked Kara May how writers do this.

'You're talking about backstory,' she said.

'Yes, OK,' I said. 'How do writers put in backstory?'

'There are lots of ways but personally I like to slip it into the dialogue,' she replied.

'What's that again?' I said.

'The talking bits.'

'I'm not planning on putting many talking bits in,' I said.

'Well, then I suppose you could weave it into the text.'

'The bits that aren't talking?' I said.

'Yes.'

'So I asked you how writers write backstory and you're telling me they write it in the writing?'

'Yes,' she replied.

Which just goes to show that talking to writers isn't always a good way to find out about writing. So I'm just going to persevere with my lists. Here are three other things you need to know:

1. My best friend is called Khoi. We mostly get on but he shows off a lot. Khoi's dad is called Minh and works for AardvArk, which is the most amazing company and makes computers, tablets, phones, consoles, games and smartwatches.

2. For his last birthday Khoi got an AardvArk smartwatch, which is pretty cool. Even Mr Adams who takes us for PE doesn't have one and he loves gadgets. Plus he's a grown-up so he can just buy the stuff that he wants rather than having to wait for his birthday.

3. The lollipop lady who helps us safely across the road to school is called Bettina. Mum said Bettina has issues (which is another way of saying she's always grumpy). My sister misheard this and thought that Mum said 'tissues', so she's always asking Bettina if she can have one for her runny nose. Bettina's main issues are that she has a strong dislike of parents, children and cars, which makes you wonder why she decided to become a lollipop lady in the first place.

I'm learning that the problem with writing backstory is that it's easy to get distracted and overload it with details. Like that stuff about Agnes mishearing 'issues' as 'tissues'. It's not really got anything to do with the story. Agnes's random behaviour is much more significant, which brings me to four reasons why my sister is random:

1. Agnes has imaginary friends. Yes, that plural 's' is intentional. Agnes has so many imaginary friends I think even she has lost count.

2. Agnes's imaginary friends are all monkeys. They first materialized after a visit to the zoo. Mum is quite patient with her but I can tell from the way Dad talks about it that he shares my feelings on the subject. He was the one who suggested a second visit to the zoo, hoping we could abandon the imaginary monkeys there, but Agnes just collected more. Spend any time with her and you'll notice her watching them. When we're inside they sit on the bookshelf, or hide under tables and tickle her toes. Outside, they're usually found swinging from the trees, jumping on cars or shinning up window cleaners' ladders.

3. Agnes finds her imaginary monkey friends hilarious. The problem is that since they are invisible (because they don't exist) all everyone else sees is a little girl pointing at a tree or a car or a window cleaner's ladder, laughing her head off and calling out things like, 'Hey, Captain Wiggles, what are you doing up there?' and 'Little Lara Long-Tail, get off that car!' and 'Now, Arnold Bulk, you know you'll burn your tail if you go in there, don't you?'

4. She blames all her naughty behaviour on the monkeys and says things like, 'I was late because Mrs Bullworth made me watch her whole tap dance routine' and 'It wasn't me that picked next door's flowers, it was Jemima Jumping Bean' and 'Old Musty Face, why did you use Hector's shoes to scoop up the yogurt?'

When you write a lot of lists you find one list often leads on to another list or reminds you about something else you need to list. For example, reading that last list reminds me that I haven't explained why my mum flooded the kitchen with yogurt.

So here are four of Mum's inventions that haven't made any money ... yet:

1. The Yogurt Tap. This was a superficially simple idea that came from a time Agnes and I were demanding more yogurt and Mum responded, 'Oh, I suppose I'll just turn on the yogurt tap, shall I?' My mum's invention ideas are often inspired by things like this. Then she starts lightbulbing (which is a word she made up) and she goes distant while she designs her invention. The problem was that yogurt doesn't smell all that delightful after it's been stuck in a tap for three hours on a warm summer's day. Also, the yogurt solidified and blocked the pipe so Mum had to increase the pressure, which is why yogurt splurged all over the kitchen floor.

2. The Smart Umbrella. How often have you been walking along with an umbrella only to realize that it isn't raining any more? That has actually never happened to me, but nevertheless it was the question that got Mum lightbulbing. Her idea was that the umbrella would know when it had stopped raining and close. The problem was that the one thing worse than foolishly holding an umbrella when it's not raining is having the umbrella suddenly shut on you, trapping you inside.

3. The Hover Key Ring. Mum was always losing her house keys in her bag, but one day she realized that you only really need your house keys when you're at your house, so why not leave them there all the time? Except you can't leave them in the door, can you? What if they were in the right place while also being totally out of reach? So Mum created a key ring that made her keys fly up to the roof until summoned. Unfortunately the ring got hooked around the TV aerial and the keys got stuck on the roof.

4. The Thinking Cap. This one was actually quite cool. It was a cap with a light bulb attached to the top. She got the idea from getting an idea for something else. She was lightbulbing when she wondered if it was possible to make a hat with a light that came on when the wearer had an idea. It worked by reading the brain activity of the wearer. The problem with this one, even though it worked pretty well, was that Mum couldn't think of a use for it and so it remained on a shelf in her workshop.

I'll tell you about more of Mum's inventions later but now we should continue with the actual story, which began with a challenge.

Chapter 3
The challenge

'I'd like you all to come up with a theory then write how you could prove it,' said Mr Pickering (who was both our teacher and the deputy head). 'For example, I have a theory that Hector has a long explanation about why he was yet again late this morning. I can prove my theory by asking him why he was late.'

This wasn't the first thing Mr Pickering said that morning but Kara May told me that I should experiment with using more dialogue in my story and possibly even try beginning a chapter with some talking. I am not convinced this is a good idea because if I were reading this I would be thinking:

1. Who was he saying it to?
2. Where was he when he said it?
3. When did he say it?

The answers to these questions are:

1. He said it to the whole class.
2. We were in our classroom.

3. He said it on Monday morning, 10th February, the day that Khoi 'called challenge'. (I'll explain what that means in a minute.)

Since the important bit about the challenge happened at break time I'm going to skip through the first lesson with a list of five things that happened in class after Mr Pickering talked about his theory:

1. I told Mr Pickering that I was late because Bettina, the lollipop lady, had got into a big row with a motorcyclist and refused to let us cross until he apologized, which took ages.
2. Mr Pickering said that it was my mother's duty as a parent to get her children to school on time and told me he would be having a word with her.
3. Once the whole Embarrassing Hector business was done with, the lesson settled down and we all had to come up with theories – as well as ideas for how we could prove our theories.
4. I struggled to come up with anything good.
5. Khoi came up with the theory that in the future we would be able to communicate with each other

telepathically. Mr Pickering thought this was an excellent theory but was less convinced by Khoi's way to prove it. He just wrote: 'Wait and see how AardvArk solve it.'

Once the lesson was over, it was break time and Khoi came up with our challenge. Here are eight things that led to it:

1. Khoi and I were hanging out together as usual and Khoi was going on about his telepathy idea and how it was actually possible and that his dad had sat in meetings about it.
2. I said I didn't think it sounded very likely.
3. Khoi said I didn't understand technology.
4. I said I did because my mum was an inventor and only last week she was designing a device to put the crunch back in your cornflakes after they had gone soggy.
5. Khoi said that was a stupid idea and that real inventions these days weren't like that. They involved things like his smartwatch, which could translate ninety languages into English.
6. I secretly agreed with this but Khoi was annoying me so I said, 'She is a real inventor. She just hasn't

made any money out of her inventions yet. And anyway, she could have worked for AardvArk but she turned your dad down when he offered her a job.' (Which was true.)

7. Khoi said, 'He only offered her a job because he felt sorry for her.' (Which wasn't true.)

8. At this point I started shouting that this wasn't true and about my mum being cleverer than his dad. I didn't actually believe this but the argument had got the better of me and a bunch of other kids had gathered around so quite a few people heard Khoi say, 'OK then, I call challenge.'

I should probably explain that if ever Khoi and I have a dispute over something, one of us will 'call challenge' to decide who will be proclaimed victor. To give you an idea of what this usually involves, here are three challenges we have previously called:

1. Khoi's claim that ants can run three times faster than centipedes was settled in a purpose-built arena (a cardboard box). The result was inconclusive because at no point did we persuade the contestants to run in the same direction.

2. My belief that 'the smaller the ball, the bigger the

bounce' was put to the test by dropping various balls out of Khoi's downstairs window. The result was that I was wrong. There is no connection between size of ball and bounciness.

3. Khoi called challenge on the question of who could go the longest without blinking. I won two of the agreed three staring matches and was declared the victor, but I suspect that he would have won the next one. It is really hard not to blink, especially when your sister is running around teaching her monkey choir all five parts to her song, 'Blinking is Fun'.

So Khoi suggested we set a challenge to prove that his dad was better than my mum.

'Better at what?' I asked.

'Everything,' said Khoi. 'Your mum can't even get you to school on time. We live about the same distance from school and I'm never late.'

'So you want a race to school?' I said.

'Yes. The quickest person to school is the victor,' said Khoi.

'No,' I said, because even in the heat of the argument I knew I didn't actually have a chance of winning. I was just trying to defend Mum. I realized that I needed a way of setting a challenge that neither of us could win. 'The victor is the one who gets to school in sixty seconds flat.'

'A minute?' exclaimed Khoi. 'But that would involve travelling at a constant speed of ninety miles an hour.'

'That's the challenge,' I said, offering my hand. 'The school run in sixty seconds. Maybe your dad's not up to it but my mum is.'

I was hoping he would refuse but Khoi shook my hand and said, 'Challenge accepted,' then the bell went and we filed back into school.

Chapter 4
Lightbulbing

I hoped it would turn out to be just a bit of playground chat like that time we agreed to have a party at the top of Mount Everest in the year 2050. We're not really going to do that. Mount Everest is REALLY high and we'll be REALLY old then. Definitely too old for parties.

However, while Khoi, Agnes and I were waiting to be met by our parents at the end of the day, Khoi said to me, 'I've started working out on my smartwatch ways we can cut down delays caused by traffic lights and pedestrians.'

'There's a thirty-mile-an-hour speed limit,' I said.

'Yes, that's a problem,' said Khoi. 'Dad won't do anything illegal. I know that because I once asked him to hack into the school computers and give us an extra day's holiday. Dad refused to do it because it was against the law.'

'Well then, you won't be able to do it,' I said, hoping to draw a line under the whole business.

Unfortunately several pieces of bad luck coincided to ensure that the challenge was still on:

1. Mum arrived and asked, 'What are you two talking about?'
2. Khoi told her about the challenge.
3. Khoi's dad arrived to pick up Khoi. (This was extreme bad luck. Khoi's dad is usually far too busy being important, but he had a conference call later that day or something so was working from home.)
4. Mum told Khoi's dad about the challenge.
5. Khoi's dad chuckled and said, 'I think we have an unfair advantage. Rob takes your car to work, doesn't he?'
6. Mum said, 'You think you can beat us?' and offered her hand.
7. Khoi's dad shook it.

Our parents had hijacked our challenge, which was annoying because I could tell that Khoi's dad didn't even think it was possible. Whenever Mum and Khoi's dad talked it was like that bit in cowboy films where the cowboys look at each other and you see their eyes up close and hear twangy-whistly music.

Mum didn't speak as we set off home. I could tell she was lightbulbing.

The walk home was always better than the walk there because we weren't in a hurry, but it was still annoying that we had to cross the road with Bettina. There was already a crowd of people jostling around near the crossing so we had to queue up just to get near the kerb. Bettina was arguing with an ice cream van driver, telling him he had to turn his music off. The ice cream van driver was insisting that it was his legal right to play music. Bettina said it was disturbing the peace and, if he was going to play it, he should at least find something more interesting than 'Greensleeves'.

When we finally stepped on to the crossing she yelled, 'Yes, come on, quickly and safely across now. I can't stand here all day.'

'She's so rude,' said Mum.

'Mum, be quiet,' I said. 'No one talks back to Bettina. Remember that time we saw her chasing a car because the driver complained she was making him late for work?'

'Someone has to tell her,' said Mum.

'Yes, but not us,' I said. 'Please keep quiet.'

Mum did as she was told but Agnes tugged Bettina's coat.

'Excuse me,' she said. 'Have you got a tissue for Graham Grizzle? He's caught a terrible cold from a gorilla called Colin.'

'Keep moving,' cried Bettina. 'No pulling my coat. No talking while crossing. Get to safety. Go.'

Halfway between school and our house is a cafe where we sometimes stop. I have mixed feelings about this. These are three reasons I like stopping at the cafe:

1. Mum sometimes lets me have a strawberry milkshake.
2. Mum sometimes lets me have a Chocolate-Explosion muffin.
3. Occasionally I get both a milkshake *and* a muffin, which is what I call a jackpot day.

Now for three reasons I don't like stopping at the cafe:

1. Agnes also likes milkshakes but thinks it's hilarious to blow them back through the straw, splattering me.
2. Agnes also likes Chocolate-Explosion muffins but she gets bored about halfway through and starts picking her muffin apart and then squishing it

together. This is very messy but mostly I object to it because it puts me off the muffins.

3. Agnes often talks to her imaginary monkeys in a loud voice, which is embarrassing. Mum says I'm oversensitive to this kind of thing but even she gets embarrassed when Agnes includes rude comments about the other cafe customers while telling off her monkeys.

Here are five things Agnes has shouted out in the cafe:

1. 'Hey Sergeant Tring, stop bothering that man with the horrible shirt.'
2. 'No, Madam Noodle, I don't think that lady is interested in having a haircut, although she does look like she needs one.'
3. 'Jimmy Krink, please stop bothering that man talking loudly on the phone.'
4. 'Yes, Zolulah, that boy's nose is rather runny, isn't it? I'll ask Bettina for a tissue next time I see her.'
5. 'Malcolm Flump, that lady is not wearing a tea cosy. It's just a hat that *looks* like a tea cosy.'

Perhaps you think some of these comments sound funny but that's only because you don't have to sit there while the people in the cafe turn to stare at you or walk over to your table to tell your mum that she has a very rude daughter and demand apologies.

I'm surprised we're still permitted to enter the cafe. If I worked there I wouldn't let people like us in. I would tell us we were bad for business. But the lady who works there (whose name is Olga) doesn't seem to care. In fact it's worse than that. She actually finds Agnes funny and hoots with laughter whenever she overhears one of her comments. Nor does she mind wiping up her splattered milkshake with a cloth, and when she sees what Agnes has done to her muffin she simply says, 'Ah, your little one is being creative again. Just like her mother.' Olga thinks my mum is great because she has one of her few inventions that works, although it says a lot about my mum that she never got paid for it. Or rather, she never got paid in money.

'Special salad?' Olga said as we sat down at our usual table.

'Lovely,' said Mum. 'It's still working then?'

'You can judge when you see the salad,' said Olga.

Mum designed the Automatic Salad Maker (or ASM) for Olga. You place all the ingredients in it, such as your lettuce leaves, tomatoes, cucumbers and dressing, then you close the door and press a button. When you open it, the cucumber has been diced, the tomatoes sliced and the lettuce washed. The whole thing comes out in a bowl with the perfect amount of dressing on it. It's pretty amazing really. Obviously, I'd prefer it if it made Chocolate-Explosion muffins or anything more exciting than salad but you can't have everything.

When I asked how it worked, Mum said it 'realigned the molecules of the ingredients', which meant nothing to me. This was the thing about Mum's inventions. Sometimes they seemed silly (I mean, a yogurt tap, really?) but the technology behind them was always pretty mind-blowing.

I was hoping the ASM would actually make some money but Mum had already moved on to the next invention. 'It's not The Big One,' she told me. 'The Big One' was how she referred to the invention that would change everything and actually make money.

Agnes and I drank our milkshakes while Mum waited for her salad. I knew she was thinking about the challenge because Mum thinks out loud. It's often kind of mumbly and sometimes so quiet it sounds like humming but it's never just in her head like normal people's thinking.

'Cut out traffic ... up and over ... most direct route ... remember to factor in wind direction ... One minute, one minute ... must be possible ... '

I needed to say something. 'Look, Mum, there's no point thinking about it. It's impossible to get to school in under a minute. Totally impossible. It's ridiculous to even try.'

'Not at all,' said Mum. 'Your school is roughly a mile and a half from our home so—'

'We'd have to travel at ninety miles an hour,' I interrupted. 'Which would be illegal.'

'Not necessarily.'

'Dangerous, then,' I said.

'Yes, we'd have to minimize the danger. Safety first.'

'Please, Mum,' I said. 'Please forget the challenge.'

Before Mum could respond, Agnes started chasing one of the monkeys around the cafe, screaming, 'Not the sugar. Don't eat the sugar, Marty Make-up! You know how you get when you eat sugar!'

The other customers looked alarmed by the sudden disturbance and Mum decided it was time to take us home, so asked to have her special salad to go.

Chapter 5
Dad's job

When we got home, Mum went straight down into her workshop in the cellar while Agnes said she had some 'important monkey business' to take care of in her bedroom. I watched a bit of television then decided to go and see what Mum was up to. When I opened the cellar door I could hear three things:

1. The radio. Mum always listens to the radio when she is working but only ever to a radio station on which bored-sounding journalists read the news or 'not funny' comedians do 'not funny' comedy or interviewers interview angry people who have been overcharged for their electricity bills.
2. Hammering.
3. Mum mumbling about her ideas and talking to the bored-sounding people on the radio. It sounded like this: 'So all I need to do is work out the correct trajectory, taking into account the ... Of course you'd say that, but not everyone has the same privileged background as you, do they? ... I'd have to factor in the wind speed and direction I suppose.

Oh, hello Hector. It's a fascinating problem you've set me.'

'Hi Mum,' I said. 'What are you doing?'

Mum turned to face me. She had a pencil behind her ear and another in her hair. 'Let me show you. Where's my pencil? Oh, here's one,' she said, picking up a third pencil from the desk and grabbing a piece of paper. 'Look.'

She drew two dots on the piece of paper. 'Say that point A is our house and point B is school. Our usual journey involves travelling around buildings, waiting at crossings and avoiding other pedestrians.' She drew a wiggly line between the two dots to demonstrate. 'All these diversions increase our total journey considerably. What we need is to travel directly, as a crow would travel.'

'A crow?' I said.

'Yes, and how do crows avoid all these obstacles?'

'They fly.'

'Exactly. They fly.' She threw the pencil. It missed the piece of paper and bounced off the desk.

'Fly to school?' I said.

'Yes, like this. Look.'

Copy of Mum's Diagram on How

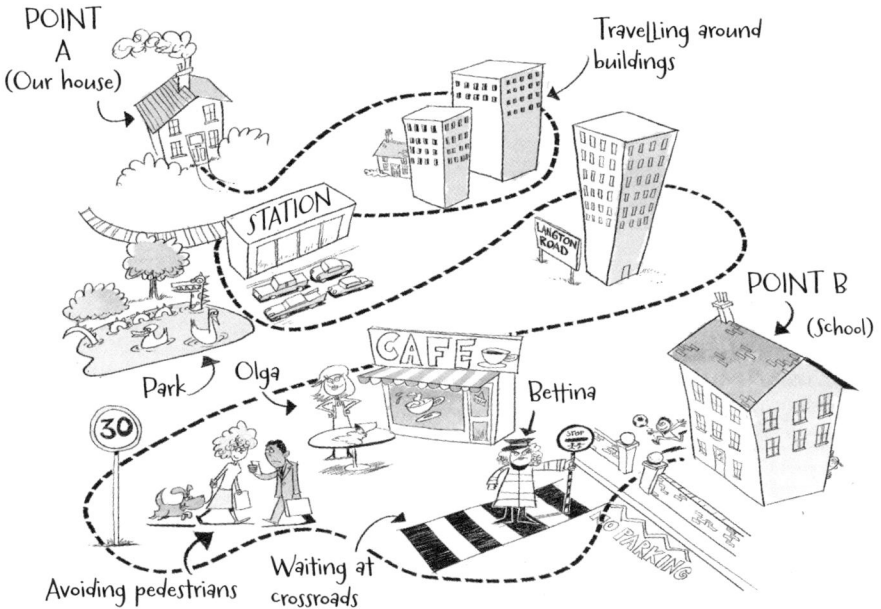

POINT A (Our house)

Travelling around buildings

STATION

LANGTON ROAD

POINT B (School)

Park Olga

CAFE

Bettina

30

Avoiding pedestrians

Waiting at crossroads

STOP

NO PARKING

She showed me a picture of my bed flinging me out of the window, then me parachuting into school.

'No way,' I said. 'That's way too dangerous. You can't just fling your children out of the window, parachute or not.'

Mum met my eye and I saw it slowly sink in that I was right. She scrunched up the piece of paper and threw it away.

'Early workings,' she said. 'But I'll come up with something. I promise, it will be completely safe. Well,

to Get to School in Sixty Seconds

as much as anything is completely safe. After all, they say crossing the road is one of the most dangerous things you can do and we have to do that every day on our usual journey. Anyway, time for some clean-desk thinking.'

Mum swept her arm over the desk, clearing piles of diagrams, pencils and half-made bits of machinery so that they clattered to the ground. I took this as my cue to leave. I went upstairs and headed for the kitchen.

Agnes came bounding into the room looking even stranger than normal. Here are three reasons my sister looked strange:

1. She had a cardboard box on her head with eyes cut out and the words ANTI-BRAIN-REEDING-HELLMIT.
2. She was wearing one of Dad's horrible cowboy shirts.
3. She was carrying two coat hangers bent out of shape.

'What are you doing?' I asked.

'Me and my monkeys have been working on this. What do you think?' She tapped her box hat with the hangers.

'It's amazing,' I said. I was being sarcastic but she doesn't understand sophisticated humour like sarcasm.

'It's to stop people reading my brain.'

'Yes, I guessed that. There's only one e in reading.'

She threw me a quizzical look. 'How do you know how I spell reading?'

'It's written on your hat. One of the e's should be an a.'

Agnes looked up to try and read it but noticed one of her monkeys and said, 'Hey, Gerald Hoppykins, what are you doing on the stairs?' Then she wandered out again.

Here are six things that happened after that:

1. I made cheese and tomato sandwiches for Agnes and me.
2. I found a packet of crisps for us each.
3. I poured us each a glass of orange squash.
4. Agnes and I watched television while eating our sandwiches and crisps and drinking our orange squash.
5. We went upstairs and brushed our teeth.
6. I checked Agnes had got to bed and then went to bed myself.

Throughout all of this Mum did not emerge from the workshop, where she was hammering, soldering, welding and talking to the radio, saying things like, 'Try funding it if you want it to function properly.' Agnes and I were used to falling asleep to the sound of hammering but there was another bang I was listening for – the sound of the front door and Dad coming home. The rule was that if I was still awake when he came back I was allowed to get up and say hello, so I always listened as hard as I could for this bang. This is a list of three things I look at in my room while waiting for Dad to come home:

1. My glow-in-the-dark stars, arranged in the actual positions of real constellations.
2. A triangle of yellow light made by the street lamp shining through the gap in my curtain.
3. Something that flashes in one of my boxes of stuff. I have no idea what it is. It must be some toy I've forgotten about but I can't believe it still has batteries that work because it's been flashing for years. I've never been bothered to check.

I fell asleep before hearing my dad come in. Here are three things I like about my dad:

1. He is funny. No one can make me laugh like my dad. Agnes finds him funny because he holds her upside down, trying to shake out the silliness but really making her feel even sillier than before. But with me he knows I like cleverer humour like actual jokes and sarcasm.
2. He knows a lot of things and can answer almost any question. Mum says it's because he works in sales and is good at sounding convincing but whenever I check what he has said on the Internet he is right.
3. He makes a really good Sunday roast. It's the only

meal he ever really cooks and it always takes him ages in the kitchen, with crackly jazz music playing, but the results are good. His Yorkshire puddings are as big as boats and his roast potatoes are super flaky delicious.

Now, here are three things I don't like about my dad:

1. His job, because it means we never see him in the week.
2. His job, because it makes him really stressed.
3. His job, because he argues with Mum about it sometimes. She says that if he hates it so much he should leave it. He replies that he can't leave it because money doesn't grow on trees.

I fell asleep thinking about all this.

Chapter 6
The helicopter room

Here are five things you notice when you wake up to find that your bedroom has been converted into a helicopter:

1. Having a bedroom window open, even just a little bit, causes quite a lot of chaos and some of your favourite posters become ripped beyond repair.
2. Birds do not expect bedrooms to be in the air and sometimes fly into the windows.
3. Pyjamas are not adequate to keep you warm once you are airborne.
4. It is hard to get dressed while wearing a seat belt.
5. The propellers make a lot of noise and you need helmets with headsets to hear what is being said.

I sat upright and immediately sensed something tugging on my shoulder. I looked down to see a seat belt holding me in place.

'Smart seat belts,' said Mum. 'They adjust to your position.' Her voice was coming through a speaker in a helmet I was wearing.

I turned around to see her sitting at my desk, except now it had a large joystick in the middle and a couple of new levers. Also, the window no longer looked out on our back garden. Now, on the other side of the window pane there were only clouds ... and the occasional pigeon.

'What was that?' I yelled, as something hit the side of my room with a THUD.

'Just a pigeon – I can see it on the under-room webcam. It doesn't look very happy, but it's all right.' Mum looked over her shoulder at me and smiled. 'So? Do you like it?'

'Do I like what?' I exclaimed. 'The fact you've turned my bedroom into a helicopter? No, not really. When you said you'd come up with something else, I didn't think you meant this.'

'It's much safer than the bed-fling idea,' said Mum. 'I've converted your cushions into airbags, your desk now doubles up as a console and I've installed fire extinguishers in your cuddly toys drawer.'

'I don't have a cuddly toys drawer,' I said.

To be clear, I do not have a cuddly toys drawer.

'Well, whatever you keep in it, that's the fire safety area now. The emergency exits are your bedroom door, the window and the secret escape hatch under your bed. See, totally safe.'

'How did you do all this overnight?' I asked. 'My room is part of the house.'

'Oh, I made all of the rooms detachable last year. Remember, when I had an idea about a house in which the rooms kept changing where they were? I called it the Shuffle House.'

I remembered it. Dad had got out of the bath, opened the door and found himself on the doorstep wearing a towel, while Agnes's room opened into the kitchen, making it all too easy for her band of outlaw monkeys to make off with a whole packet of biscuits.

'Where's Agnes?' I said.

'She's in the top bunk, of course.'

'I don't have a top bunk,' I said, but when I looked up I saw that I did indeed have a top bunk. I don't know why I was so surprised. When you have the sort of mum who converts your bedroom into a helicopter to fly you to school, why would you be surprised that she had engineered you a bunk bed overnight?

Agnes leaned over the edge so her head appeared upside down. She was wearing a pair of goggles, a flight hat and a long scarf that dangled down to the floor.

'Flight Commander Squiggles has lost control,' she yelled. 'Abandon ship, abandon ship.'

'Agnes, don't be silly. It's not a ship. It's a Room-copter. Or Heli-room. I can't decide which sounds more impressive,' said Mum. 'Anyway, I need to concentrate. We're coming down.'

'Down where?' I asked.

'On the school roof of course,' said Mum. 'I can hardly land outside in the street. They have those big zigzag no-parking lines.'

Chapter 7
Mr Monk

Parents, pupils and teachers stared up as Mum landed the Heli-room. The wind from the propellers made hats fly off and everyone's hair flap around wildly. Some of the smaller children burst into tears but most people just stared in disbelief. The only person who didn't seem at all surprised was Mr Monk. He stuck his head out of a window, looked up and said, 'I'd better get the ladder.'

Here are five things you need to know about Mr Monk:

1. Mr Monk gets very annoyed when people call him a school caretaker because his official title is Onsite Maintenance Manager.
2. Mr Monk takes care of the school.
3. Some people think Mr Monk is grouchy.
4. I don't think Mr Monk is grouchy. I think he's probably quite lonely because his wife died a few years ago and so he lives on his own now.
5. Mr Monk likes to state the obvious.

Here are four obvious things he said while getting his ladder and helping us down:

1. 'I'm not sure this roof was designed to hold a bedroom.'
2. 'Most people arrive on the ground.'
3. 'They blow quite a gale, those propellers.'
4. 'I suppose we'd better get you down.'

I changed into my school clothes, then Mr Monk rescued us. After that, we were told to go straight to Mr Pickering's room. (Not the classroom but a special room he gets because he is the deputy head as well as being my teacher.) Agnes went straight to her class.

On the way to the room, Mum said, 'I thought the landing was a little bumpy. What did you think?'

'Possibly it was a little bumpy,' I agreed. 'Also, I think you may have crushed a chimney.'

'Yes, well, you can't make an omelette without breaking some chimneys, can you?' replied Mum.

You're probably thinking, *Wow, he sounds a bit relaxed about his mum doing such a ridiculously irresponsible thing.* You're probably imagining how angry you would be if your mum did something like that. But I was used to it. Here are three ridiculously irresponsible things Mum has done:

1. She turned the stairs into a slide.
2. She put a jellyfish in the bath.
3. She made a Speedi-Grow Formula that enlarged a boa constrictor to six times its normal size while I was in the house. The first I knew of it was when the giant snake spat an apple at my bedroom window.

Looking at that list, I'm worried it puts Mum in an even worse light so I've added some explanations:

1. The stair slide was one of Mum's solutions to making the house more fun – but the truth is that slides are fun on the way down but actually quite tricky on the way up.
2. The jellyfish in the bath is a bit harder to explain, but Mum told me that it wasn't poisonous and there really wasn't anywhere else to keep it and besides, it wasn't bath night or anything. When I asked her why she had it in the first place, she simply said, 'Jam jars, of course, darling.'

3. Yes, I realize the snake thing sounds far-fetched. A giant snake is more the kind of thing you read in a book about wizards. What can I say? It happened. Mum's inventions often seem like flights of fancy but she talks about them in a way that makes them seem perfectly ordinary. She explained that nature was perfectly capable of making small things grow bigger. There was nothing magic about it. Science often involved trying to imitate what happens naturally. I accepted this just as Kara May accepted the fifty pounds Dad gave her to replace the chunk of apple tree that the giant snake devoured before the formula wore off and the boa constrictor shrank down to a more manageable size.

Now for the bit where Mr Pickering summoned us to his room to tell off Mum.

'Now, Mrs Cook—' began Mr Pickering.

'Cooper,' said Mum. 'I never took my husband's name.'

'Right, well, Mrs Cooper—'

'Ms.'

'Ms Cooper, you really can't land a helicopter on the school roof.'

'Why not?' asked Mum. 'There are no parking restrictions on the roof.'

'That is because it is a roof,' said Mr Pickering, 'and I think it is reasonable to assume that people won't park on it.'

'That's because they don't have a Heli-room,' said Mum, 'or Room-copter. Which do you think sounds better?'

'Personally I like the sound of a normal method of transportation that doesn't involve landing on our roof. I mean, what if everyone turned rooms into helicopters?'

Mum laughed. 'Sorry, but that's not very likely.'

Mr Pickering did not laugh. Instead he crossed his arms and glared.

'If I had sorted out the trajectory and really given it some welly, I think I could have done it.'

'Done what?' asked Mr Pickering.

'Got to school in sixty seconds flat,' said Mum.

'Why would you want to do that?' asked Mr Pickering. 'Just leave on time. I mean, most parents are content to drive.'

'Cars are bad for the environment,' said Mum. 'My Heli-room is completely green. We have a solar panel on our roof that powers it.'

'Please, Ms Cooper—'

'Call me Sally,' said Mum.

'I'd rather not,' said Mr Pickering. 'Please could you deliver Hector to school in a normal, safe way? What about setting off on time and walking? That's environmentally friendly and it keeps you fit.'

'Walking,' said Mum with a faraway look in her eyes that could only mean one thing. Mum was lightbulbing again. 'Yes, walking.'

'So?' said Mr Pickering. 'Can we agree, no more flying bedrooms?'

'Certainly not,' replied Mum, 'I never repeat ideas.'

'Thank you,' he said.

'No. Thank *you*,' said Mum.

Chapter 8
Breaking eggs

My first lesson was disrupted by the sound of the Heli-room taking off again. It was really loud and yet Mr Pickering refused to stop speaking, meaning no one had any idea what his instructions were and the class was in total chaos until he repeated it all again, by which time the lesson was almost over.

At break, a bunch of kids gathered around to hear about my journey to school, asking things like:

1. 'What was it like being in a flying bedroom?'
2. 'Did you really knock a bird out of the sky?'
3. 'Can your mum turn my bedroom into a helicopter too?'

I didn't really want the attention so I gave them the most boring answers I could manage:

1. 'It was all over before I knew it, really.'
2. 'A bit but it was fine.'
3. 'No.'

Khoi tried to get them interested in his attempt to make it to school in sixty seconds, but no one cared about the traffic app on his smartwatch or wanted to hear about his algorithms.

After they had gone, he said, 'It makes no sense. I'm talking about the sort of technology that can really change the world. And yet all they care about is your mum's silly helicop-room.'

'Heli-room,' I said. 'I suppose algorithms aren't as interesting as actual moving, flying things.'

'They will be when I win the challenge.'

'It's not about that,' I said. 'The challenge is to get to school in sixty seconds and that's clearly impossible. We might as well call it quits.'

'Dad won't do that,' said Khoi. 'He's really competitive.'

'So is my mum, unfortunately,' I replied.

'I don't know why she doesn't just come and work for him. He's asked her enough times and she'd actually make money then.'

'I know,' I said miserably. 'She'll never do it though.'

'Why not?'

I made a list of the reasons in my head:

1. Mum doesn't like Khoi's dad. I'm not going to list all of the words she has used about him (even though Kara May said I should be honest with the language I use) but the top three are: smarmy, big-headed and conceited (which means being in love with yourself).
2. Mum doesn't want to work for 'the man'. When she first said this I assumed she was talking about Khoi's dad but it turned out that 'the man' isn't a particular man but a phrase that means she doesn't want to work for a big corporate company.
3. Mum thinks AardvArk is slick and soulless, which means that it makes things that work and look good. Her inventions work but always look like something cobbled together from stuff she's found in our house – or the actual house itself.

After break, the day settled down into a pretty standard Tuesday, which in itself is probably one of the most standard days of the week. It involved:

1. English
2. Maths
3. continuing our project about foxes.

After school I met up with Agnes and we waited for Mum. We were used to her being late to collect us, but today I had to deal with all the stares and whispers from the other parents who had seen me arrive that morning. Agnes spent the whole time trying to arrange her imaginary monkeys into an orderly line. When Mum did arrive I didn't recognize her at first because:

1. She was wearing a yellow boiler suit.
2. She had a beekeeper's hat on.
3. She was driving a car.

There was often something unusual about Mum's appearance so, rather than asking about the boiler suit or the hat, the first thing I said was, 'Whose car is this?'

'It's Mrs Slouka's car, our neighbour,' said Mum. 'I lost track of time and it was outside with the keys in so I borrowed it. Come on, hop in.'

'You've stolen a car?'

'Borrowed,' said Mum. 'Get in.'

I got in the passenger seat, while Agnes got in the back.

'No, Mr Militrix,' said Agnes. 'You can't make an omelette ... Yes, I know there are enough eggs but they have already been cracked so we can't use them.'

I would have dismissed this as more of Agnes's nonsense had it not been for the smell. I looked in the back of the car and saw shopping bags, one of which had tipped over. A box of eggs must have been resting on top because the whole of the back of the driver's seat was covered in yellow and white gunk.

I pulled my seat belt on. 'Mum, do you remember that in-car cleaning device you invented?'

'The car-pet cleaner,' said Mum. 'I always thought that was a good name. Yes, I remember it. What about it?'

'We're going to need it,' I replied.

Chapter 9
Flapjacks

When we got back I ran to Mrs Slouka's door and rang the bell. A female police officer answered the door. Mrs Slouka had called the police. Of course she had. She had arrived home with a carload of shopping, carried Baby Marky in, then come back for the shopping only to find that someone had driven off with her car. Luckily the police officer didn't arrest Mum because:

1. Mrs Slouka didn't want to press charges.
2. The police were well aware of my mum's history and her scatty ways.
3. The police officer had more important things to do.
4. The police officer thought Mrs Slouka was a bit careless leaving her car unattended for so long with the keys in the ignition.

After issuing warnings to both Mrs Slouka and my mum, the police officer left. I was relieved. We had been to the police station before and it was never fun.

Here are three reasons why Mum had been in the police station before:

1. She had to explain about the incident with the giant snake and Kara May's apples. (No one really believed this story and it didn't help that Kara May makes things up for a living. Luckily, in the end, she dropped the charges and turned the whole incident into a book.)
2. A passer-by had thought we were burgling our own house when we were just trying to retrieve Mum's keys from the roof.
3. She had to explain how she infected the local water supply with yogurt.

The last time we were there, the desk sergeant said that Mum's file was so big it counted as a dangerous weapon, although I suspect this was a joke as these days everything is kept as computer files and they don't actually weigh anything.

After promising to clean the car, we returned to our house. On the way round, Mum stopped to snap off a branch of Kara May's apple tree that overhung our garden.

'Mum,' I said, 'that's not yours.'

'I think you'll find it's legal to chop it off if it overhangs your property, so long as you offer it back,' said Mum.

'Are you going to offer it back?' I asked.

'What would Kara May want with a lopped-off branch from her own tree?' said Mum. 'Besides, I've asked her before. She doesn't mind.'

We went into the house. 'So, Hector, do you want to see tomorrow's plan?'

'Seriously, Mum,' I pleaded, 'there's no need. You heard what Mr Pickering said.'

'I did. He said we should walk. Come and meet Tony.'

She disappeared down into the cellar leaving me with two choices:

1. Follow her.
2. Don't follow her.

I was considering these options when Agnes dashed past me. 'Sorry, Hector,' she said. 'The monkeys say there's something amazing down there.'

She charged down the steps, then let out such a big gasp that I had no choice but to follow her. When I reached the bottom of the stairs I saw why.

Mum was feeding Kara May's branch to an ant the size of a small horse.

I'll say that again.

Mum was feeding an ant the size of a small horse.

Yes, I know that sounds like the sort of thing you would see in the kind of unbelievable film they show on Bank Holiday mornings, but what can I say? It's true. Besides, I told you about the snake. All of this stuff sounds incredible and then my mum makes it sound ordinary. OK, maybe not ordinary but possible.

'Hector, Agnes,' she said. 'This is Tony.'

'Tony?' I said.

'Yes, as in Ant-tony,' said Mum. 'Antony.'

'Does he bite?' asked Agnes.

It was a silly question since Tony was in a tug of war with Mum over the tree branch.

'Is he dangerous?' I asked, nervously.

'He's a vegetarian,' said Mum.

'How do you know?' I asked.

Tony won the fight and made short work of the branch, shredding it with his pincers and guzzling it down.

'Because I offered him a chicken sandwich earlier on and he showed no interest.'

'Mum, why is there a giant ant in our cellar?'
I asked.

'He's an experiment,' said Mum. 'Do you remember my Speedi-Grow Formula?'

'How could I forget?' I asked.

Instead of answering my question, Mum extracted a pencil from her top pocket. She was about to write something down when Tony snatched it out of her hand with his pincers and devoured it.

'I was thinking how our journey to school would be a lot longer if we were much smaller. For Tony here, our journey to school would be the equivalent of us driving to Wales every day – I mean, when he's his normal size.'

'Except Tony is an ant so he doesn't need to go to school,' I said.

'Or Wales,' said Agnes.

'There's no need to be silly,' said Mum. 'Besides, the formula is about to wear off. In five, four, three, two, one ... Here we go.'

Right on schedule, Tony shrank back down to the size of an ant, scuttled around in a few hurried circles then vanished between two floorboards.

'Oh, I liked him big,' said Agnes. 'I thought we could ride him to school.'

'Ride a giant ant to school?' said Mum. 'Don't be silly. Ants aren't nearly fast enough. Also, they're very hard to steer. Besides, Tony was just an experiment. Or rather, an experim-ant.' Mum laughed at her pun even though it wasn't funny. People often mistake puns for jokes. Puns are not jokes. They are wordplay. They deserve groans not laughs.

'Mum,' I said. 'This formula is The Big One. It's incredible. I mean, terrifying, but still incredible. There must be a way to make money out of this. Surely.'

'No, it's far too unstable,' said Mum. 'You saw how quickly the effects wore off. But it will help us win the challenge.'

I'd had enough. 'Why can't I have a mum who has a normal job and takes us to school and brings us back in a normal way and, in her spare time, bakes flapjacks rather than making rooms fly or enlarging insects? Dad would agree with me if he was here, but he never is because of his stupid job.'

I turned around and stormed up the stairs but as I went up I heard Mum mutter, 'Flapjacks?'

Chapter 10
The three-step plan

I am a heavy sleeper. I can't tell you how many times I've woken up to discover that I've fallen out of bed without noticing. This is a list of things I've managed to sleep through:

1. Deep-tunnel drilling – Mum has drilled so many holes under our house that if you look at it from the outside, you can see that it is about thirty centimetres lower than it used to be.
2. Car alarms (set off by the drilling).
3. Doorbells (rung by neighbours coming round to complain about the drilling and the car alarms).
4. Mum and Dad arguing loudly (about the drilling, the car alarms and the neighbours).
5. Agnes singing loudly about monkeys.

On this particular Wednesday morning, though, I slept through Mum lifting me out of bed, dressing me, then placing me on the outside lawn. It was only when a sprinkler came on that I jumped up to find myself standing in my back garden.

'What's going on?' I demanded.

'You have to stand very still,' said Mum. She was standing in front of me wearing a hard hat, the yellow boiler suit, and knee and elbow pads.

'Why do I have to stand still?'

'Because if you don't, you might crush something,' said Mum.

'Crush what?'

'Our house,' said Mum. 'Now, stay still and don't panic.'

'Why would I panic?' I asked, immediately panicking.

Mum patted me on the arm. 'You trust me, don't you?' she said breezily. 'I tried it out first myself, so there's no need to worry.'

'Is this about the helicopter room?'

'No, I'm just telling you not to panic because I'll be with you the whole time that the Speedi-Grow Formula is working.'

'You've given me the Speedi-Grow Formula?' I exclaimed.

'Trust me, Hector. It's going to be fine.'

She positioned herself behind me and placed a hand on my shoulder. Before I could ask anything more, I felt something so strange it is difficult to describe. The thoughts that ran through my head were:

1. *Everything is shrinking.*
2. *Why is everything shrinking?*
3. *Hold on, no. Everything isn't shrinking. I am growing.*
4. *Mum really has given me the Speedi-Grow Formula.*
5. *Why would she do that?*

Sudden growth is weird and not all good. I made a list of things I felt and showed it to Kara May and she said it seemed very negative considering that growing really large is an incredible thing to happen. Kara May said that good writing was fun to read and suggested I make a new list that sounded more positive. After some thought I came up with this list of four fun things about suddenly growing massive:

1. I felt a bit like the giant in *Jack and the Beanstalk*, although I never once felt the urge to say 'Fee' or 'Fi', let alone 'Fo' and 'Fum', and I certainly didn't smell anyone's blood. Eurgh.
2. A man walking his dog in the park was so distracted by seeing me that he walked straight into a pond.

His dog was really excited that his owner had finally seen what fun it could be splashing in ponds and jumped around happily.

3. A duck that had been sitting in the pond suddenly took to the air to avoid the man and dog, only to be faced with the even more alarming sight of a gigantic human (me). Luckily it dodged me and found somewhere quiet to go and have a lie down (or do whatever ducks do after they've had a fright).

4. For a brief moment, when all the confused shouting below was lost under the howling of the wind, I felt a moment of calm. It was as though seeing the world from such a height put everything into perspective. The feeling didn't last long but I still think about it now sometimes.

'Mum?' I said, turning around.

'Stay still,' she replied, her voice as quiet as a mouse in my ear. Out of the corner of my eye I could see her tiny hand on my massive shoulder. 'Keep your head forward,' said Mum. 'You'll need to walk very carefully.'

But I was still growing and was now so large that I was pretty sure my feet were going to smash through our garden fence. I raised my right foot.

'Balance,' said Mum.

'What?' I replied.

'As soon as you reach maximum height you'll only have a few seconds to make it to school in three steps. Your first should be coming down in the station car park, but watch out for the commuters. Your second footstep should reach that patch of land behind the flats on Langton Road. Your third should get you to the road in front of the school. Be really careful not to step on any of your school friends.'

I felt a sharp jab in my chest. 'What was that?' I said, wobbling.

'Just a pigeon,' said Mum.

'A pigeon?' I cried.

'Yes. It's fine. It's flown round you. Now, please try to concentrate. You just knocked the washing line over.'

It was certainly one of the strangest experiences of my life. I could see people in the streets below, pointing. I could hear them shouting and car horns beeping but as I grew and grew, something strange happened to the sounds. It reminded me of the effect on the car radio when we drive through a tunnel. I saw more pigeons swerving to avoid me. The wind rushed through my ears. Above, I could hear the sound of engines. When I looked up I saw a low-flying toy plane. Except it wasn't flying low and it wasn't a toy. It was a full-sized plane. And I was enormous.

'Don't worry,' she said, 'you're almost at the peak of your height.'

'How big am I?' I asked.

'Er … very! You should be about 1483 metres,' she replied. 'You see, I wanted to see if you could do the trip to school in three strides. I calculated that a step of 76 centimetres was not an unreasonable ask, and since your normal height is 140 centimetres, all I had to do was times your height by 1059. Then I worked out where you could step without crushing anyone. Now, get ready for the first step.'

Mum shouted all of this but I could only just hear it. By now my ears were full of the whistling wind, the roaring planes above and the city sounds below. Mum was a tiny little thing on my shoulder. She was right, though, that the station car park was perfectly placed to put my foot down in. I waited until someone had finished parking his car then placed my toe on to the tarmac. Amazingly, the person was running for the train and didn't notice. Mum says commuters never notice anything, but the ones on the other side of the platform facing the car park were staring in disbelief.

'Next step,' said Mum. 'You're already shrinking.'

Once again she was right. One minute I was worried about the dangers of getting a plane in my face, the next I was worried I wouldn't make the last two steps.

I reached the patch of land Mum had suggested, but I was getting smaller too quickly.

'Mum, I just kicked a satellite dish off a block of flats.'

'People watch too much television if you ask me anyway,' she said. 'Now, make the final step before it's too late.'

I could see the school but I wasn't convinced I could make it in one step. I had no choice but to jump. It was only a small jump. Or rather it would only have been a small jump had I been normal size. Since I was so massive it was a big jump that got me over a row of houses and landed on the zigzag lines in front of the school.

As I landed I felt a crunching thud: my feet had just made a massive dent in the tarmac. A second later and I was reduced to my normal size, with my mum still behind me. She grabbed my hand.

'Come on,' she said, 'we're in the middle of the road

and remember, crossing the road is one of the most dangerous things you can do.'

We climbed out of the crater and reached the pavement, watched by hundreds of astonished pupils and parents. Then the hole began to fill with water.

'Oh, I think you may have hit a water pipe,' said Mum, thoughtfully. 'I didn't anticipate that.'

Chapter 11
The flooded playground

We found Agnes on the pavement, splashing in the stream of water that was gushing out of the hole my landing had made.

'How did you get here?' I asked.

'Monkey magic,' she said.

'Don't be silly,' said Mum. 'Florence's mum gave her a lift. I mean, I couldn't be sure Agnes would hang on to your shoulder so I decided it would be more responsible to arrange a lift.'

'Responsible?' I said. 'How is any of this responsible?'

There was a lot of shouting that morning. Here are some of the reasons people yelled:

1. The other parents mostly shouted about the burst water pipe making them wet.
2. Mr Monk shouted that the burst water pipe had flooded the playground.
3. Mr Pickering shouted that the school would have to close until the matter was resolved.
4. Agnes shouted at her monkeys, 'You are not Singing in the Rain.'

I met Khoi standing by the gate looking at his watch.

'Oh, sixty-one seconds, bad luck,' he said.

'What?' I exclaimed. 'It was quicker than that!'

'No, Khoi's right,' said Mum. 'I didn't take into account the walk to the gate. Is your dad still here?'

'No,' he replied. 'He had an important client meeting today. Mum dropped me off. I'll definitely tell him about this, though.'

'Don't bother,' said Mum. 'The Speedi-Grow Formula is just a gimmick. Besides, can you imagine if everyone had it? There'd be chaos.'

It was easy to imagine the chaos. By now, water was spraying into the air and cascading down like rain.

School had to be cancelled, news which got a number of different reactions, including:

1. 'Hey, great, a day off!' (The pupils)
2. 'But I've got to be in the office in an hour's time.' (Half of the parents)
3. 'But I'm supposed to be going for coffee.' (The other half of the parents)
4. 'This is most inconvenient.' (Half of the teachers)

5. 'Although we could catch up on some planning.'
   (The other half of the teachers)
6. 'I wonder why monkeys can't hum.' (Agnes)

They all agreed on one thing, though: my mum was to blame. I wanted to hide, but the flood limited the number of available hiding spots.

Every parent had to take their child home. Everyone was soaking wet and furious – a bad combination. They didn't know yet but for many of them the day would get even worse because:

1. They would return to houses with no water due to the burst pipe. (Quite bad)
2. Some would have to have long angry conversations with water companies and listen to hours of hold music. (Really bad)
3. They wouldn't have water until the following day when the water companies finally fixed the pipes, meaning they wouldn't be able to wash. (Really bad and a bit smelly)

Before we went home, though, we had to have another meeting with Mr Pickering.

We sat in his room, while he tried to establish what had happened. Mum explained that she had:

1. calculated the three-step plan to the last detail
2. given me the Speedi-Grow Formula
3. stayed with me the whole time
4. been cautious when crossing the road.

The only good thing about the flood and the shutting-down of school was that it meant Mr Pickering was very busy and didn't really have time to tell us off. His parting comment was that my mother should think long and hard about what it meant to be a responsible parent.

Mum replied that his idea of a mother was probably someone who wore an apron and made flapjacks.

'I never said anything about flapjacks,' protested Mr Pickering, which was true.

'Your tone did,' snarled Mum. 'Your tone was dripping with flapjacks.'

'In which case, don't listen to my tone. Listen to my words. If there are any more of these incidents or if Hector or Agnes is late one more time this term, they will be suspended from the school and I will recommend to the Board of Governors that they should be excluded altogether.'

Mum would have had lots of things to say to that had the police not turned up at this point. Mr Pickering had called them. The fire brigade turned up too, to suck up the water. According to Khoi, that bit was fun to watch but I wasn't able to hang around, even if I had wanted to. The police needed Mum to come and answer some questions.

Everyone in school saw us get into the back of the police car. I asked Kara May if there was a word meaning 'famous, but not in a good way' and she said it was 'infamous'.

My whole family was infamous.

Chapter 12
The police station

I've noticed that I've not really stuck to my idea of writing a story entirely as lists so now I'm going to write this chapter entirely as lists.

Here are three things police officers don't like little girls doing in the back of a police car:

1. singing songs about monkeys
2. fiddling with the windows
3. going on and on about them turning the sirens on.

Four things the police officer said to my mum at the station:

1. 'We have a number of witnesses claiming they saw a giant boy this morning. They say the boy resembled your son. Do you know anything about it?'
2. 'Have you any explanation as to how the water pipe was damaged outside the school?'
3. 'Do you know anything about the satellite dishes that were knocked off roofs this morning?'
4. 'What's this on your record about a giant snake?'

Four things my mum said to the police officer in response to the four things he said to her:

1. 'A giant boy who looked like my son? It doesn't sound very likely.'
2. 'The water pipe? Yes, it burst as soon as we arrived outside the school.'
3. 'I did not see any satellite dishes being damaged on our journey to school, although I may have heard about one, now I think about it.'
4. 'My neighbour is a writer. Too much imagination, if you know what I mean.'

In response to this, the police officer said, 'I am afraid we are going to have to detain you for a little longer until we get to the bottom of all this. We have contacted your husband to come to collect the children.'

Mum wasn't happy about this but I persuaded her that, given the situation, it was best to go along with the police enquiries. After all, I didn't have much doubt about who did all the damage.

Here are six things that happened when Dad turned up at the police station:

1. He hugged Agnes and me.
2. He listened to the police officer's account of what had happened.
3. He listened to Mum's account of what had happened.
4. He checked that Agnes and I were unharmed.
5. He had a row with Mum.
6. Agnes's monkeys went out of control, making Agnes fall about in fits of giggles as they juggled police helmets and used truncheons for their spontaneous Morris Dance.

We went home after that, although Dad had to spend most of the rest of the day on the phone for the following five reasons:

1. He had to take lots of important work calls in the study with the door shut.
2. He made lots more calls to the police station, trying to get Mum released.
3. He got a pizza delivered.
4. He tried to call a plumber about the water pressure.
5. He took a number of phone calls from parents who wanted to shout at Mum but settled for shouting at him.

Four more things that happened before bed:

1. I watched TV with Agnes.
2. I made a list of reasons why this was my new worst day ever.
3. Dad managed not to lose his temper at all until Mum came in after we had gone to bed.
4. Dad lost his temper.

Nine things my parents said in the argument:

1. 'Minh's not the bad guy here. AardvArk is a good company. It's a good offer.'
2. 'I'm not going to work for the man.'
3. 'You mean like I do?'
4. 'I didn't mean that.'
5. 'Mr Pickering is right. You are an irresponsible parent.'
6. 'At least I'm there for them even if I don't make flapjacks.'
7. 'One of us has to pay the mortgage. Why are you talking about flapjacks?'
8. 'That's what it all boils down to in the end, isn't it? Money?'
9. 'We can't live like this.'

Chapter 13
Radio Monkey

The next day, Dad took us to school in the car. We set off with plenty of time to spare, which was good because our journey was slowed down by lots of workmen digging up the road to repair the pipes.

Kara May told me that it is important to 'flesh out the characters' which is another way of saying 'explain what they're like'. Dad has not appeared much in the book so far, so here are six things worth knowing about him:

1. Dad met Mum when they both worked for a company called Tech Spec.
2. After going out for two years they got married then went to Barbados on honeymoon. (There is a picture on our window sill of them wearing swimsuits and smiling.)
3. Mum left Tech Spec when I was born and she never returned.
4. Khoi's dad also worked for Tech Spec until he was headhunted by AardvArk. (Headhunting sounds to me like it involves chasing trolls through an

enchanted forest but actually it's more about phoning someone up and offering them more money to change jobs. There are lots of business phrases that sound more exciting than they are – like Blue Sky Thinking, which makes you think of a skydiver falling into floating clouds of thought whereas actually it just means people in suits thinking stuff.)

5. AardvArk also tried to headhunt Mum but she told them she wasn't interested.

6. My dad has never been headhunted, although I think he'd like to be.

On the drive to school, Dad turned on the radio. It was someone talking about which companies had made the most money this year. It was no wonder they sounded so bored.

'And in the technology sector,' said the presenter, 'it would seem there really is no catching up with industry leader, AardvArk ... '

'Shall we listen to something else?' said Dad, switching it off.

'Yay! Can we listen to Radio Monkey?' asked Agnes.

'There's no such radio station,' I said, folding my arms crossly.

'Hey, you two, be nice,' said Dad.

'When you're feeling fun and funky, tune your radio to Radio Monkey,' sang Agnes.

'There is no such station,' I stated.

'Hector,' said Dad sternly, 'don't be unkind to your sister.'

'But Dad, she's making up radio stations.'

'So?' said Dad. 'Why does it matter? What do they play on Radio Monkey, Agnes?'

'Monkey music,' she said.

Before I could say there was no such thing, Dad started singing, 'Twinkle Twinkle Little Monkey ...' which made Agnes hoot with laughter. I found it funny but I was still too grumpy to laugh.

'Old MacDonald had a monkey,' sang Dad. 'Oo-Oo Oo-Oo Oh.'

'We wish you a merry monkey,' sang Agnes.

I laughed in spite of myself and then I had an idea for one so I put aside my annoyance at Agnes and joined in. 'Row, row, row your monkey gently down the stream.'

We were all falling about laughing when Dad's phone rang and he told us we had to be quiet because it was work. Dad's phone is connected to the car so when someone speaks, their voice comes out of the speakers.

'Rob,' said a voice. 'You're not here.'

'No, I left you a message, Brian. Family emergency. I'll be in just after ten.'

'Just after ten?' said the angry-sounding man. 'The client comes in at half past. How on earth are we supposed to have a pitch ready by then?'

'I emailed you what I did last night,' said Dad. 'I think it's pretty much there … '

'Well, I'm glad you think it's pretty much there because this is an extremely important client and we can't afford to lose another one to Aardvark.'

'I know that,' said Dad. 'Listen, I've got my kids in the car.'

'And my monkeys,' chirruped Agnes.

'What was that?' said the man.

'Nothing,' said Dad. 'Listen, Brian, we're going through a tun – Starting to cut ou – See you late – '

Dad made his voice sound like it was breaking up, then disconnected the phone.

'What tunnel?' asked Agnes.

'One of your monkeys' tunnels,' said Dad.

He parked the car and I opened my door.

'Hector,' he said, 'would you mind taking your sister down? I'd really better get to the office.'

'Can't you come with us?' I said. 'We're supposed to be dropped off by a grown-up.'

'Yes, I know but … Oh, look, there's Khoi and his dad. Perhaps they can take you in.' He wound down the window. 'Hi, Minh, would you mind taking my two in with you? I'm in a bit of a hurry.'

Khoi's dad stopped by the door and smiled. 'Sure thing, Rob. The more the merrier. How are you? That was quite a stunt Sally pulled yesterday.'

'I'm fine. We're all great. As I say, in a bit of a hurry. Big client meeting. You know what it's like.'

Khoi's dad nodded but said, 'No, I'm senior management now. I leave all that messy stuff to the sales teams.'

Dad smiled in a way that I wasn't sure how to describe until I talked to Kara May about it and she told me that what I was describing was usually referred to as a 'thin smile'. That sounded appropriate. Dad smiled thinly.

We got out and Agnes immediately latched on to Khoi to tell him about monkeys, while Khoi's dad walked into the playground with me.

'How are you, Hector?' he asked.

'I'm fine,' I muttered. Then something occurred to me. 'Can you please tell Mum you'll never beat her time? I'm worried she'll try again and get into even more trouble.'

'I'll tell her next time I see her,' said Khoi's dad. 'Your mother has a brilliant mind but her inventions are too outlandish. Look at this.' He slipped off his watch. It was the same model as Khoi's. 'Such a simple thing. People have been wearing wristwatches for many years. Innovation isn't about reinventing the wheel. It's about making a wheel that works better. Here, you can have this one.'

He handed me the watch.

'I can't take that,' I said. 'Don't they cost hundreds of pounds?'

'They do,' said Khoi's dad, 'and this one is yours now. I'm upgrading today anyway.'

'I can't accept it,' I said.

'Yes, you can,' said Khoi's dad. 'And next time you talk to your mother, maybe you could show her the smartwatch – she may realize that AardvArk isn't so bad after all. She'd be a valuable asset to our company.'

'You still want her to work for you?' I said.

'Of course,' said Khoi's dad, smiling fatly. 'Sally is a first-rate problem-solver. What she lacks is the ability to see how to make her inventions fit into the world. That's where I come in.'

I had no response to that. Maybe he was right. Maybe Mum did need someone to guide her. Maybe she did need a proper job. I put on the smartwatch, deciding to keep it – for now anyway. I was glad when Mr Pickering turned up and we had to go in, because the other parents were beginning to stare.

Chapter 14
Infamous-er

If helicoptering into school had made me infamous,
growing to the size of a skyscraper made me even
infamous-er. Kara May was less happy with that
made-up word but I think it accurately sums up how it
feels when everyone in the school thinks your mum
should be locked up.

Mr Pickering was especially angry, which was unfair
because he knew perfectly well that it was my mum
and not me who caused all the problems. I could tell
he was angry with me because he didn't smile when he
said my name.

Most of the teachers avoided me, but at break time
Mr Monk came looking for me.

I was on my own when he found me because
I wanted to investigate my smartwatch without
Khoi seeing. I knew it was stupid. Khoi's dad would
probably tell him, but it felt like I was betraying
Mum and I knew Khoi would pick up on this and
enjoy making me squirm. I had found a quiet spot
behind a tree when Mr Monk arrived and said three
obvious things:

1. 'Hiding behind a tree, are you?'
2. 'Well, you can't hide forever.'
3. 'Yesterday was a bit of a day, wasn't it?'

'I'm not hiding,' I said. 'I didn't ask my mum to do all this.'

'Well, obviously not,' he said, which I thought was a bit rich coming from him.

'What do you want?' I snapped.

'Ah, well, it's a bit of a delicate matter,' he said.

'What does that mean?'

'Your journey to school,' he said, 'I mean, your normal journey, the one along the road ... '

'Yes.'

'You walk past Bettina.'

'Yes. Why?'

I was expecting him to tell me how she had held him up or whacked his car with her lollipop or something like that. Instead, Mr Monk pulled out an envelope from the inside pocket of his overalls. 'Would you mind handing her this on your way in tomorrow?'

I took the envelope. 'Is it her birthday?'

'I have no idea,' said Mr Monk. 'Why do you ask?'

'It feels like a birthday card.'

'Oh, I see, yes. It's her birthday. That's a birthday card for her. Will you promise me you'll give it to her? I think considering I spent most of yesterday mopping up your mother's mistake it's the least you can do.'

I agreed to give her the card. Mr Monk thanked me and left. The bell rang. I was walking back to class when Khoi found me. 'Where have you been?'

'I've been lying low.'

'Are you kidding? You gave everyone the day off. You're a hero.'

'I don't want to be anything. I just want to have a normal life,' I replied.

'Oh right, and who's that for, then?' he asked, noticing the envelope in my hand.

'This? The lollipop lady,' I said. 'Why?'

Khoi burst into hysterics.

'What?' I said. 'Why are you laughing?'

'Hector loves the lollipop lady,' he said, making himself laugh even more.

'No I don't. What are you talking about? What's so funny?' I asked. 'I don't love anyone.'

'So why are you giving the lollipop lady a Valentine's Day card?'

Which was the point I realized that it was the 13th of February and that tomorrow was Valentine's Day. Mr Monk had asked me to give Bettina a Valentine's Day card.

Chapter 15
Third time lucky

After school, Agnes had a play date with her friend, Florence, who was both human and non-imaginary. Florence's mum was collecting both girls in her car and had agreed to drop me off at home on her way. She offered me the passenger seat but I could see that look in her eyes and I knew I would have to spend the whole journey answering questions about Mum and what it was like to grow massive. It was less stressful to stay in the back with the random monkey chat.

Florence loved Agnes's monkeys and actively encouraged her to talk about them by asking loads of questions, including:

1. 'Where are the monkeys now?'
2. 'What was the monkey doing on Ms O'Shearer's head?'
3. 'Why is Grampy Boxley scared of heights?'
4. 'How can a roof eat nuts?'
5. 'So are there any monkeys on top of that petrol station?'

My sister's responses to these questions went like this:

1. 'The monkeys are everywhere, Florence. There was one on Ms O'Shearer's head for the whole of PE.'
2. 'Clinging on. Grampy Boxley is scared of heights and Ms O'Shearer is very tall.'
3. 'He once fell off a roof eating nuts.'
4. 'Grampy Boxley was eating the nuts. My monkeys love nuts.'
5. 'No, Florence. Monkeys are allergic to petrol. Everyone knows that.'

I was relieved to be out of the car and back home until I opened the door and heard the radio blasting, Mum humming and some kind of construction going on.

Mum was working.

I opened the cellar door and went down. Mum was leaning over her worktop wearing goggles, holding a soldering iron.

'Hi Mum,' I said.

She switched off the iron and lifted her goggles.

'Ah, Hector, this is it. I know it. This will get you to school so quickly, you'll be able to go back and pick up something you forgot and still win the bet.'

'Mum,' I said, 'you've been arrested, you've annoyed the whole school, Dad's angry with you – you have to stop. It was just a silly playground challenge.'

'I can do it,' said Mum.

'No, you can't.'

'Why not?' she snapped. 'Because I don't work for a million-pound company like Khoi's dad?'

'Billion pound I think,' I said. 'This isn't about you or him. Anyway, what's wrong with earning money? Khoi's dad works for a company that makes things people actually want!' I had half a mind to show her the smartwatch as Khoi's dad had suggested, but I thought better of it.

'So will I, when I invent The Big One,' said Mum, lowering her goggles and turning back to the worktop.

'This isn't about you,' I said. 'It's about me and Agnes, and if we are late again Mr Pickering will suspend us.'

'I know, but you won't be late again. You see, I realized I was thinking about the problem wrongly—'

'Stop!' I yelled.

Mum looked up at me, but kept her goggles on. I couldn't read her expression because her face was all mixed up with my own reflection.

'Please Mum,' I said. 'For me. Give it up.'

'Darling,' said Mum, with a sad tilt of her head. 'I have to see this one through.'

'But it's not even a challenge you can win. It's impossible.'

'I don't believe in impossible,' said Mum.

'I heard you arguing with Dad. He's right. We can't live like this.'

When Mum lifted her goggles I could see the tears in her eyes but I couldn't tell if it was because of our conversation or because of the soldering. 'This is the only way I know how to live,' she said, before lowering the goggles and returning to her work.

Chapter 16
Thought Transference Transporter

Mum was still working in her workshop when Agnes came home, and continued after we went to bed. I tried lying awake to talk to Dad, but he must have been working late because I drifted off to sleep.

When I did hear the door, I could tell from the line of sunlight around the edge of the curtain that this was the sound of Dad leaving for work. I looked at my clock. It was half past six. I wanted to get up but my body had other ideas and I fell back to sleep until the clock read: 08.30.

Half past eight! I thought. *I'm going to be late.*

I jumped out of bed, dressed and ran downstairs.

Agnes was sitting on a kitchen stool eating out of one of the cereal bowls she had laid out.

'You'll have to wait if you want breakfast,' she said. 'The monkeys are using all the bowls at the moment.'

'We haven't got time for breakfast. We haven't got time for anything. Mr Pickering gave us a warning. We can't be late for school again. They'll have us thrown out.'

Agnes turned to one of her monkeys. 'Yes, he is a bit over-excited, isn't he, Bernie Bottletop?'

'STOP TALKING TO MONKEYS!' I yelled. I didn't mean to lose my temper. I didn't mean to shout but I couldn't stand it any more. 'THEY'RE NOT REAL! THEY'RE IMAGINARY! THEY'RE IN YOUR HEAD!' I hollered.

Agnes hopped off her stool and smiled. 'Oh, I know that, silly.'

'You ... you know?'

'Yes, of course.' She looked at me as though I'd just said the silliest thing she had ever heard.

'So why do you go on about them all the time?'

'Because monkeys make life more fun.'

I have thought a lot about this since, but at the time, I did not have a response for the following reasons:

1. I had only just woken up and was still groggy.
2. I hadn't had breakfast.
3. If we were late for school we could get suspended and have to go to a school even further away.

'Agnes,' I said. 'Do you like your teacher and your class?'

'Yes.'

'Me too. So we need to get going. Get dressed as fast as you can. Don't worry about the monkeys. Get dressed and get down. We need to go.' I ran into the hall. 'Mum! Mum!' I yelled.

I couldn't hear humming, hammering, soldering or arguing with the radio.

'Mum!' I shouted.

I went down into the cellar and found her sitting staring at our shower cubicle (which was no longer in our bathroom).

'Mum, are you OK?'

I asked because:

1. She looked tired.
2. She was crying.
3. She was clutching a coconut.

'What's wrong?' I asked. 'What's happened?'

'I've done it,' she said. 'This is how we win the challenge.'

'A shower cubicle?' I said.

'It's not a shower cubicle,' she said. 'Well, it was, but it's not now.'

'Mum, that man from the water company warned you against messing about with the water. Now, we've got to go.'

'Go?' she said. 'I've only just got back.'

'What are you talking about?' I said. 'What is this thing?'

'It's a Thought Transference Transporter,' she said. 'I call it the Triple T for short.'

'Mum, we don't have time,' I protested.

'Oh yes we do. You see, how it works is that you get in, think about where you want to go and then it sends you there.'

'You mean like a teleporter?' I said.

'Exactly.'

'But that's not possible.'

'Yes it is. It works. It really works.'

'What do you mean?'

'I just tested it.'

'Mum,' I said, 'where did you get that coconut?'

She smiled, not thinly or fatly but sadly. I know that sounds odd. How can someone smile sadly? But if ever there was a sad smile, it was my mum's as she replied, 'I went to Barbados. It's where your father and I went on honeymoon.'

'But, how does it work?'

'Ah, now there's a simple question without a simple answer.'

My mum was right. Her answer was anything but simple and I would be lying if I said I understood it all but I picked up enough to form this list of how she invented the Triple T:

1. Mum has been working on a molecule transporter for years.
2. The Automatic Salad Maker (ASM) used a technique based on this. The reason it didn't need to touch the ingredients was because it was manipulating their molecules to chop, dice and toss them.
3. It had never occurred to Mum that this could be used to transport people until Agnes had wandered in with her Anti-Brain-Reading-Helmet.
4. Seeing Agnes's helmet, Mum realized that her Thinking Cap was, in a very basic way, reading her thoughts.
5. All she had to do was increase its power so that it picked up subtler differences in brain activity, then connect it to a bigger version of the salad maker and hey presto: the first ever Thought Transference Transporter.

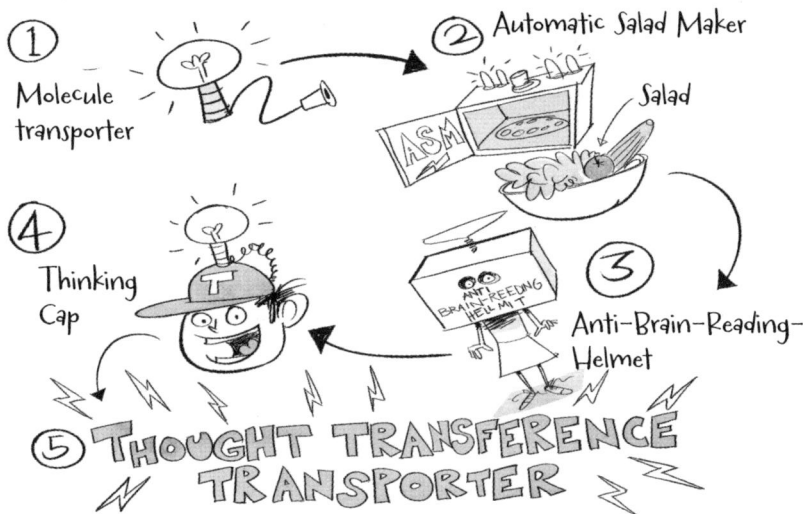

① Molecule transporter

② Automatic Salad Maker

Salad

ASM

④ Thinking Cap

③ Anti-Brain-Reading-Helmet

⑤ THOUGHT TRANSFERENCE TRANSPORTER

'Now, are you ready to give it a whirl?' said Mum.

I looked at the device. It was every bit as ramshackle and shoddy as all of her other inventions.

'Are you sure it's safe?' I asked.

'I told you, I tested it myself,' said Mum. 'All you have to do is think really hard about where you want to be.'

I looked at the clock on her wall. It was 08.43. It was too late to walk. We had missed the bus. We could still drive and get there in time but Dad had taken the car and I doubted Mrs Slouka would ever lend Mum her car again.

We had no choice. 'Agnes,' I yelled. 'Are you ready? We need to go NOW!'

Chapter 17
A last resort

It took Mum a few minutes to prepare the machine, so it was 08.49 by the time Agnes and I were standing in the shower cubicle waiting to go.

Agnes was singing quietly to herself:

'La la la, do do do, that's the monkeys' song.
Do do do, la la la, they sometimes get bits wrong.
La la do, do la la, the monkeys are such fun.
Do la do, la do la, the monkeys cannot hum.'

'Agnes,' I said. 'Please, for once, can we forget the monkeys? We really need to concentrate for this to work.'

'That's right,' said Mum. 'You both need to think about the same place.'

'How precise does it need to be?' I asked.

'I'm not sure. But to be on the safe side, maybe think about a specific point. What about the tree at the back of the playground?'

'Yay,' said Agnes. 'Up the tree.'

'No,' I said firmly. 'Next to the tree.'

'Oh.' She sounded disappointed but I didn't care. I didn't want to take any more risks.

'What will happen if there's already someone standing there?' I asked.

'You'll materialize next to them,' said Mum. 'Seriously, Hector, you worry too much. It's completely safe.' She turned a dial and the machine began to hum and whirr. 'Are you ready, kids?'

'We're ready,' said Agnes.

'The tree at the back of the playground,' I said.

'Don't say it. Think it,' said Mum.

I thought about the tree. I thought as hard as I could. I tried to picture its rough bark and high branches. I tried to imagine every detail about it. I'd spent the previous day hiding behind it so I had a pretty good image of it. The machine buzzed into action and I felt a sharp wind pick up and whirl around me. I gripped Agnes's shoulder. I would be lying if I told you I wasn't nervous but it had got to the point where I couldn't imagine anything worse than being late for school again. So it was worth the risk of the Thought Transference Transporter splitting us into little bits and scattering us all over the place if there was a chance we would make it to school on time.

What happened next is difficult to describe because:

1. It didn't feel like anything I had ever experienced before.
2. It didn't look like anything I had ever seen before.
3. It only took a second.

Kara May told me that the above description wasn't good enough so I have done my best to describe how it felt being transported by the Thought Transference Transporter. These are some of the things that I felt:

1. tickly toes
2. pins and needles (all over)
3. itchy palms
4. as though my head was being squashed
5. as though my arms and legs were being stretched
6. dizziness
7. a blinding flash of light
8. a rattling sound like a metal hamster running around a metal wheel inside my brain.

Reading that back, it sounds awful, which it would have been if it had lasted for very long, but it was all over so quickly that I barely noticed it before it had stopped. Then I opened my eyes.

'Monkeys!' gasped Agnes.

'Agnes!' I responded, feeling the fury bubble up inside me. I was furious for the following reasons:

1. We were not in the playground.
2. There were three actual real-life monkeys staring at us as though we had just appeared out of thin air.
3. It was Agnes's fault.

Reading this bit back, it occurs to me that I have not been very clear about the situation. Kara May said it was very important to describe the situation in a way that means the reader understands fully what is going on. She said I should write about what was happening in terms of all fives senses, which are:

1. smell
2. sight
3. sound
4. taste
5. touch.

The only taste I had was one of feeling sick. That was because our situation felt, looked, sounded and smelled like we had been transported into a monkey cage in the zoo.

Chapter 18
Smart throw

Agnes told me later that she had tried really hard to think about the tree at the back of the playground, but that every time she had, she had pictured a monkey on one of the branches, until all she was thinking about were monkeys.

I don't know why the Thought Transference Transporter went with her thoughts rather than mine. Mum has suggested the following possibilities:

1. Agnes thought about monkeys harder than I thought about school.
2. Agnes's thoughts were louder than my thoughts.
3. My thoughts drifted at precisely the wrong moment.

Whatever the reason, it transported us into the cage, which was bad because:

1. Monkeys are territorial and do not like intruders.
2. The monkey cage is designed to keep the monkeys in so it was impossible to escape from.

3. Monkeys make a horrible screeching noise
   when human children magically appear in
   their cages.
4. Monkey cages don't smell very nice.

'These ones aren't in my head, are they?' said
Agnes, quietly.

'No,' I said. 'I'm pretty sure these ones are real.'

'I don't like these ones as much as the ones in my
head,' said Agnes.

'I did like them more than the ones in your head
until we were transported into their cage,' I replied.

'What do we do?'

'We need to get the zookeeper's attention.'

There was a woman in a brown zoo uniform outside
the cage. Unfortunately:

1. She was busily feeding the penguins.
2. The penguins were being entertaining, meaning she
   was totally focused on them.
3. There was a wire fence between us.
4. Every time Agnes or I made any noise, it attracted
   the attention of more monkeys.

'Hector,' said Agnes, 'I think I've gone off monkeys.'

The monkeys were screeching and chattering but the zookeeper wasn't looking round. The monkeys were being cautious about approaching, for the moment. Agnes grabbed my hand. She was scared. I needed to protect her. She might have been the most random person on the planet and this might have been all her fault but I was her big brother. I needed to do something. But what? I compiled a list in my head. I needed to do something that was:

1. quick
2. effective
3. smart.

I felt Agnes's hand on my wrist, touching the strap of my smartwatch. My smartwatch.

Smart, I thought. *That's it.*

'Agnes, let go.' I pulled my hand away and lifted my watch. I pressed a few buttons. The functions flashed by:

1. WEATHER
2. TRANSPORT

3. INTERNET

4. GAMES

5. CALL

I clicked on Call but there were no numbers. I tried to select Internet, thinking maybe I could find a number for the zoo but the screen flashed up NETWORK UNAVAILABLE.

'Hector,' said Agnes. 'That monkey is throwing stuff.'

One of the smaller monkeys was picking up little sticks and lobbing them at us. The others were watching intently to see what we would do.

I looked at the zookeeper, still occupied with the penguins. She was obviously used to the monkeys making so much noise. I slipped the watch off my wrist, took aim and threw it. It soared through the gaps in the fence and bounced loudly off the bucket of fish.

Finally, she turned round and saw us.

Chapter 19
Magic monkey tea

This is a list of what happened after we got the attention of the zookeeper:

1. The zookeeper looked confused.
2. She called for help on her walkie-talkie.
3. She distracted the monkeys with food.
4. More zookeepers arrived.
5. They opened the cage and got us out (without any monkeys being harmed).
6. We were taken to the office.

In the office the head zookeeper offered us seats and sat down to talk to us. He told us his name was Mr Young, which was funny because he must have been at least sixty years old ... if not older. He opened a tin, allowed us to take one biscuit each, then closed the lid again.

'I'm a bit confused about how a couple of schoolchildren came to be standing in the monkey cage with no signs of a break-in,' he said.

I had a mouthful of biscuit so I let Agnes explain. She told him that we were transported there by magic monkey tea.

'Magic monkey tea?' said Mr Young, disbelievingly. 'All right, so where did you get this magic monkey tea?'

'It comes from the Himalayas,' said Agnes. 'But we get ours at the supermarket.'

Mr Young shook his head and turned to me. 'How did you get into the monkey cage?' he asked.

'She's right. It was the magic monkey tea,' I said.

'Stop talking about magic monkey tea!' yelled Mr Young.

'You keep asking about it,' I replied. 'I'd rather forget the whole experience. In fact, I think I'm still in shock. I feel quite weak. Don't you, Agnes? Feel weak?'

'Definitely,' replied Agnes. 'I might faint.'

Mr Young gave us each another biscuit but he was obviously unconvinced by our explanation so he went on to ask the same question of how we came to be in the cage to the following people:

1. Mum (on the phone)

2. Angela, the school receptionist (also on the phone)
3. The zookeeper who I threw the watch at (not on the phone)
4. Mum (again), when she arrived to pick us up.

Their answers went as follows:

1. Mum said, 'It was a molecular shift caused by the amplification of cognitive activity, of course. Did you say "zoo"? I'll come straight away. Agnes must have been thinking about monkeys again.' (Mr Young wrote this down on a piece of paper that he stared at for some time afterwards.)
2. Angela on reception said, 'Who is this? What monkeys?'
3. The zookeeper replied, 'I've already told you everything I know. One minute I was feeding the penguins, the next something hit my bucket.'
4. The second time he asked Mum, she began to answer in the same way when Agnes interrupted with, 'I already told you, it was magic monkey tea from the Himalayas and the supermarket.' Mum smiled and said, 'Yes, that's it. It was magic monkey tea from the Himalayas and the supermarket.'

Eventually the head zookeeper gave up asking and Mum drove us to school in Mrs Slouka's car. This time there was no shopping in the back and she promised me she had got permission to borrow it.

When we got to school Agnes went straight to her class, while I went into PE. Mum went straight into a meeting with Mr Pickering. PE is never relaxing but this lesson was even worse than usual because I spent the whole time worrying.

Here are three reasons why I was worried:

1. I fully expected to be pulled out of class by Mr Pickering and suspended because we were late again.
2. I was concerned Khoi would notice that I had a broken smartwatch and ask where I'd got it and what had happened.
3. Mr Adams might notice that I wasn't really concentrating on the game of dodgeball we were playing because I was so worried.

However, Mr Pickering did not pull me out of class. When Mr Adams asked me my reason for being late, I said that we had car trouble and everyone accepted it. I didn't want to tell anyone about Mum's latest invention or the fact that I had been inside a monkey cage at the zoo that day. I just wanted to blend in (like a chameleon) or disappear (like I was invisible). Or even better, blend in *and* disappear (like an invisible chameleon).

Then I saw Mr Monk.

Mr Monk! In all the drama and excitement of the morning I had completely forgotten about his Valentine's Day card for the lollipop lady. As I caught his eye I tapped my back pocket. It was still there.

'Ah, Hector,' he said. 'Uneventful journey to school this morning?' he asked.

'Er, yes ... '

'And did you, er ... ' His cheeks turned red. 'Did you deliver the card?'

'Oh, that,' I said. 'She was in a bit of a rush this morning so I thought I'd give it to her this afternoon.'

'Oh, well, thank you then,' he said. 'That's very good of you. Blimey, I feel a bit, you know, a bit jittery. Still, nothing we can do now but wait, I suppose. I say, that's one of those AardvArk smartwatches. Are they as good as people say?'

'It has its uses, yes,' I said.

I left Mr Monk and found Khoi fiddling with his watch. 'Hello,' I said.

'Hi Hector,' he replied. 'What happened this morning?'

'You know, the usual nonsense,' I said, shrugging as casually as I could manage.

'Dad told me he gave you a smartwatch,' said Khoi. 'Do you want to connect them up so we can play Zombie Smash-Up together?'

'No, thanks,' I said, pulling my sleeve down to hide my broken watch. 'Remember your theory about telepathy?' I said. 'Do you really think it's possible?'

'I asked Dad about that. It turns out that even AardvArk are years away from making it work. The human brain is really complicated. You'd have to develop the technology that could read brain waves.'

'What about something that not only reads brain waves but that could transport someone to the place they were thinking of?' I said. 'Have you ever heard of anything like that?'

Khoi laughed. 'No. Some things really are impossible.'

'Yes. You're probably right.' I smiled. (Not thinly, fatly, sadly or happily but *secretively* because I knew something he didn't.)

After school, as Agnes and I waited for Mum to arrive, Agnes didn't mention monkeys once.

'Good day?' I asked.

'The best day ever,' she said. 'We had to write a story and I wrote about how we ended up in the zoo this morning.'

'Agnes, I'm not sure we should be telling people about that.'

'My teacher said I had a very active imagination.'

'Good.'

'I did make a lot of it up. I made it so we arrived in the penguin enclosure. I love penguins now. They're less scary than monkeys. And they are much more tuneful.'

I didn't argue. Mum eventually arrived on foot and we set off home.

'I'm so sorry,' she said.

'About transporting us into a life-threatening situation?' I said.

'I meant about being late, but that too,' she said. 'We'll obviously need to do a lot more testing on dual flights. From now on we'll go one at a time. But you have to admit, it will speed up your journey. Minh will have to say I'm the challenge victor now.'

This wasn't the first time I had wondered which one of us was the parent and which was the child.

Mum and I walked along together while Agnes skipped ahead talking to penguins.

'You can't tell him,' I said.

'But the challenge—' said Mum.

'Forget the challenge. This is the one, Mum. The Big One. The Triple T is the most amazing invention ever. Think about it. No more aeroplanes, cars or boats polluting the planet. Anyone can be anywhere in less than a second. It's going to change the world. This is the one you've been waiting for.'

'Do you really think so?'

'I know so,' I said.

We reached the crossing. I pulled out the crumpled card from my back pocket and held it out.

'You may cross now but please no dilly-dallying,' said Bettina.

'Could I have a tissue for Sir Tootalot?' asked Agnes. 'He's a penguin. He caught a cold from a polar bear called Colin.'

'What are you talking about?' snapped Bettina. 'I do not have tissues. There are no penguins. Who is Colin?'

'Bettina,' I said. 'This is for you.'

'What is it?'

I handed her the card. 'It's from someone who likes you,' I said.

This confused her but she took the card and helped us cross the road without another word. About halfway home, Mum suggested we pop into the cafe. Mum and I sat at a table, while Agnes rounded up her penguins.

'Do you really think the Triple T is The Big One?' asked Mum.

'It definitely is,' I said. 'It's amazing.'

'So what should I do now?'

'You need to talk to Dad,' I said. 'He knows how to sell things. You know how to make things.'

'Special Salad?' said Olga.

'Yes please,' said Mum. 'And strawberry milkshakes and Chocolate-Explosion muffins all round.'

Over our food and drinks, Mum and I discussed how we needed to preserve the secret of the Triple T until she knew what the next stage was. We were still talking about it when we got home and found Dad already there, sitting on the sofa, clutching a card and looking miserable.

'What's wrong?' asked Mum.

I went into the kitchen to find a snack but I could hear their conversation. I learned that:

1. Dad had got fired from his job because of being so late for work.
2. Dad didn't care that he'd been fired because he should have quit years ago.
3. Mum felt responsible.
4. Dad didn't hold her responsible.
5. Dad had got her a Valentine's Day card.
6. She had forgotten to get him one so she gave him a coconut instead.
7. This made him smile. (Kara May asked me to add an adjective here and, after thinking about it, I think the right one is 'joyously'.) Dad smiled joyously.

Chapter 20
How this story ends

I wanted to end the story there but Kara May said it needed another chapter to answer all the unanswered questions. According to her these are:

1. Why didn't Mr Pickering carry out his threat to suspend us?
2. What happened with Dad's job?
3. What happened with Mum's invention?
4. How do I feel now it's all over?
5. What happened with Bettina and the Valentine's Day card?

I'm going to take these questions one at a time, so first up, why didn't Mr Pickering suspend us? Mum got called into his office. I don't know what they talked about but he never mentioned it again.

As for Dad's job and Mum's invention, those two questions have to be answered together because he and Mum have started a company to develop the Triple T. The bank was a bit reluctant to lend them any money until Mum demonstrated how the machine worked by transporting the bank manager into her own bank vault. Now Mum and Dad have all the money they need to set up the company.

This means they are both working a lot but it also means that Dad is his own boss and he lets himself start work after he has taken us both to school. He's always been better in the mornings anyway. Sometimes we drive but usually we walk, always allowing sufficient time for the journey. Mum picks us up after school. I wish I could tell you that she's never late any more but this is supposed to be a true description of what happened.

The Triple T works but we don't use it because we have to keep it top secret. If someone at AardvArk (or another rival company) got wind of what we were doing they would try to buy Mum and Dad's company or send spies to find out how it works. Instead, Mum tells anyone who asks that she is working on a machine to make flapjacks.

The Triple T will change everyone's journeys but I don't think I'll use it to get to school even once it is available. I really like walking to school with my dad and Agnes. We always have funny conversations on the way, and Bettina isn't half as grumpy as she used to be, now that she's engaged to marry Mr Monk. He's a lot happier too. All the teachers say so but no one knows about the part I played in it. And of course, Mr Pickering is also a lot happier now that I'm always on time.

Khoi hasn't changed, though. He's still a show-off, always going on about how amazing his latest AardvArk stuff is. I can't wait to see his face when Impossible Monkey unveils the Triple T. Oh, I forgot to say: that's what Mum and Dad named the company. Dad suggested it and Mum liked it because she said it was a reminder that nothing was impossible. They asked Agnes and me what we thought. Agnes wanted it to be Impossible Penguin, but I thought about what Agnes had said about monkeys making the world more fun, so I voted for Monkey.

***

When Kara May read this she said that it sounded like the right note to end on, but I wanted to add a bit about the lists. I said at the beginning that I wanted to write a book entirely as lists but, looking back, I haven't done that. There is loads more dialogue and description than I had planned. I don't know why. It just seemed right when I wrote it. Kara May said this was fine because, even though some readers would be disappointed, you can't make everyone happy all of the time. The truth is I don't write so many lists any more. I don't worry about making sense of things as much as I used to. When your mum is the inventor of the greatest invention of all time and your sister is a super-random penguin emperor, it's better to go with the flow.

About the author

I have written lots of books about all sorts of subjects including ninja meerkats, steampunk pirates, dragon detectives and pet defenders. One of these books (*The Considine Curse*) was lucky enough to win *The Blue Peter Book Award* in 2012. I also write songs inspired by my books, which I perform when I visit schools.

The idea for this book came from conversations with my eight-year-old son, Herbie, on our walks to school. He came up with some of the unusual ways of getting to school and he even read and edited an earlier version of the book (with help from my wife, Lisa). Our daughter, Autumn, did not contribute ... but she *is* the randomest person in the world.